VIRGO:

A COMPLETE GUIDE TO THE VIRGO ASTROLOGY STAR SIGN

Sofia Visconti

Contents

INTRODUCTION

Welcome to the realm of astrology, an age old practice that has captivated humanity for generations. At its core it is a belief system that suggests a connection between celestial entities like planets and stars, and human lives. It proposes that these bodies' positions at one's birth can offer insights into their personality traits, strengths, weaknesses and life path. The heavens are divided into twelve sections in astrology called zodiac signs. Each zodiac sign is associated with its own set of personality traits and characteristics.

Within the pages of this book we embark on a journey of one zodiac sign. Virgo, the sixth sign. The objective of this book is to provide readers with an exploration into the world of Virgo. Whether you're someone intrigued by the Virgo sign or a Virgo yourself this book aims to offer you an understanding and appreciation. One that celebrates this fascinating and complex astrological sign.

Within these pages you will discover;

- **Historical Roots;** Embark on a journey through the history of Virgo. Discover its origins and evolution. In addition we will be exploring its impact on cultures and civilizations throughout time.

- **Cosmic Blueprint;** Dive into the core qualities and characteristics associated with Virgo ranging from their ruling planet Mercury, to their connection with Earth.

- **Compatibility;** Understand how Virgo interacts with other zodiac signs. Learn about compatibility and dynamics in relationships.

- **Virgo in Today's World;** Explore how Virgo traits manifest in society including their roles in career paths, family dynamics, personal growth and much more.

- **Practical Guidance;** Discover advice and helpful tips tailored specifically for Virgo individuals. Learn how to harness your strengths and manage weaknesses. In addition, learn how to navigate life's challenges successfully.

If you happen to be a Virgo seeking an understanding of your traits or if you're simply intrigued by the complex network of celestial forces this book warmly welcomes you to embark on a fulfilling journey. One of self discovery and exploration into the realm of Virgo.

VIRGO ZODIAC SIGN OVERVIEW

- **Date of Star Sign**: August 23 - September 22.
- **Symbol**: The symbol for Virgo is the Virgin. It is represented by a young woman holding a sheaf of wheat. This symbolizes purity, fertility and the nurturing qualities associated with the sign.
- **Element**: Earth. As an Earth sign, Virgos are generally characterized by their grounded nature, practicality, and stability.
- **Planet**: Mercury, the planet ruling communication, intellect, and learning, governs Virgo. This planetary influence is reflected in the intellectual and analytical abilities often found in Virgos.
- **Color**: Virgo is often associated with earthy, muted colors. Emphasis is on shades of green and brown.

COMPATIBILITY

Virgos are most compatible with other Earth signs (Taurus and Capricorn) and Water signs (Cancer, Scorpio, and Pisces). They share a practical and grounded approach to life with Earth signs and a strong emotional connection with Water signs. More on this later!

PERSONALITY TRAITS

Virgo is ruled by Mercury, the planet of communication and intellect. This contributes to the sign's analytical and detail-oriented nature. Individuals born under the Virgo sign are known for their practicality, precision and dedication. Here are some key personality traits associated with Virgo:

- **Analytical**: Virgos have a sharp, analytical mind. They excel at analyzing complex situations and solving complex problems.
- **Practical**: They are highly practical and grounded individuals. As such they often focus on the tangible and realistic aspects of life.
- **Organized**: Virgos have a strong sense of order and cleanliness. They appreciate structure and strive for neatness and efficiency.
- **Nurturing**: Virgos have a nurturing side. They often take care of others. As such they are reliable friends and partners.
- **Modest**: Virgos tend to be modest and unassuming. They don't seek the limelight and are content to work behind the scenes.
- **Intellectual**: Mercury's influence grants Virgos a love of knowledge and a strong intellectual curiosity. They enjoy learning and can be excellent problem solvers.

STRENGTHS

- **Attention to Detail**: Virgos excel in tasks that require precision and attention to detail. Thus making them reliable and thorough workers.
- **Analytical Thinking**: Their ability to analyze situations helps them make well-informed decisions.
- **Organization**: Virgos are great at creating order out of chaos and thrive in structured environments.
- **Loyalty**: They are dedicated and loyal friends and partners. As such they can be counted on in times of need.
- **Practicality**: Virgos' down-to-earth nature allows them to navigate real-world challenges effectively.

WEAKNESSES

- **Overcritical**: Virgos can be overly critical, both of themselves and others. This can lead to perfectionist tendencies.
- **Worry-Prone**: They may have a tendency to worry excessively.
- **Shyness**: Some Virgos can be reserved and introverted, making it challenging for them to open up to others.
- **Difficulty Delegating**: Due to their desire for perfection, Virgos may struggle to delegate tasks to others. Sometimes they take on too much themselves.
- **Inflexibility**: Their strong desire for order and routine can make them resistant to change.

Welcome once again to the captivating realm of Virgo! This introductory chapter sets the stage for delving into the intricacies and often misunderstood nature of this personality. We've established that Virgos astrological period spans from August 23 to September 22. We showed how it is symbolized by the Virgin and influenced by the Earth element. This imbues them with a practical disposition. Mercury, as Virgos ruling planet bestows upon them brilliance and acute attention to detail. While Virgos possess strengths like precision and loyalty they are not exempt from weaknesses such as their inclination towards perfectionism and worry.

As we venture deeper into this book you can anticipate uncovering more aspects of Virgo's personality. Along with exploring their compatibility with other signs and receiving practical guidance on navigating life as a Virgo. In the chapters ahead you'll find a thought provoking exploration of the Virgo zodiac sign brimming with valuable insights, practical guidance and a newfound admiration for this captivating and multifaceted sign.

CHAPTER 1:
HISTORY AND MYTHOLOGY

In the tapestry of the zodiac, Virgo is a constellation that holds a wealth of history and mythology. As we dive into this chapter we embark on a journey through time exploring its origins and evolution. We will also discover its impact on modern astrology. Additionally we will meet figures born under the sign of Virgo. Furthermore we will trace how perceptions of Virgo have evolved over time. From its origins to its interpretation in modern astrology. Come along with us as we delve into the history and mythology of Virgo.

THE HISTORY OF VIRGO

The constellation known as Virgo has a history that goes back thousands of years. It originated from early observations and recordings made by ancient civilizations.

- **Babylonians**; The Babylonians were one of the first civilizations in the world to observe Virgo. They associated this constellation with Shala, a goddess symbolizing fertility, abundance and harvest. It held great significance for them.

- **Ancient Egypt**; In Ancient Egypt Virgo was linked to Isis, a goddess representing fertility, motherhood and healing. The appearance of Virgo in the night sky was considered a sign for the flooding of the Nile River. This was and still is a crucial event for agriculture.

- **Ancient Greece**; Renowned for their contributions to astronomy and mythology the ancient Greeks identified Virgo as Demeter. She was a goddess associated with agriculture and harvest. Demeters connection to changes and planting cycles added depth to their perception of this constellation.

- **Roman Mythology**; The Romans adopted much of Greek mythology; thus Virgos association with Demeter continued within culture. However they also connected Virgo with Ceres, the equivalent to Demeter.

- **Ancient Chinese Astronomy**; In Ancient Chinese astronomy the constellation known as Virgo was not considered an entity but rather part of a larger constellation called "the Weaving Girl" or "Zhi Nü." This constellation represented a princess, in weaving, symbolizing craftsmanship and dedication.

- **Islamic Astronomy**; Islamic astronomers had their own interpretations of Virgo. They are often referred to as "the Lady," symbolizing purity and fertility. Some Islamic star maps depicted the constellation holding a sheaf of wheat.

- **Native American Astrology**; Native American tribes had their understandings of celestial patterns and it is possible that elements of Virgo were incorporated into their cosmology. However specific records detailing their interpretations are limited.

- **Other Cultural Perceptions and Representations**; Over the years many other cultures depicted Virgo in their star maps with variations. However they all recognized its association with fertility, agriculture and the natural cycles.

Throughout the course of history the presence of the Virgo constellation has been a source of inspiration. It symbolizes the bond between humanity and the natural cycles that govern our world. Its depiction in mythologies and cultural interpretations reflects how vital agriculture and the changing seasons have been.

The perception and understanding of Virgo has evolved significantly over time. In ancient civilizations, Virgo was primarily associated with fertility, agriculture and mythology. As cultures transitioned into the Middle Ages and the Renaissance, astrologers began to explore the personality traits and astrological attributes associated with Virgo.

In modern astrology, there has been a shift from purely mythological interpretations to psychological and personality-based insights. Modern astrologers analyze Virgo in terms of its personality traits, strengths, weaknesses and compatibility with other signs. This shift reflects a broader movement in astrology towards self-awareness and personal growth.

NOTABLE HISTORICAL EVENTS

Throughout history many significant events have taken place during the Virgo season. While astrology does not necessarily determine or predict events we can analyze some occurrences during this time for their potential astrological significance.

- **Autumnal Equinox;** The Virgo season signifies the arrival of the equinox in the Northern Hemisphere indicating the transition from summer to fall. This shift is associated with themes of balance, introspection and preparation for the months

- **Harvest Festivals;** Many cultures celebrate harvest festivals during the Virgo season. This highlights the importance of harvests and our Earth's abundance. These celebrations align with Virgos qualities. Nurturing nature.

- **Martin Luther King Jr.'s "I Have a Dream" Speech;** One of the most iconic moments of the Civil Rights Movement in the United States occurred during Virgo season. Dr. Martin Luther King Jr. delivered his famous "I Have a Dream" speech during the March on Washington for Jobs and Freedom, a pivotal event in the fight for civil rights.

HISTORICAL FIGURES BORN UNDER THE VIRGO SIGN

Numerous influential historical figures were born under the sign of Virgo each leaving a mark on history;

- **Mother Teresa** (August 26 1910); Mother Teresa symbolized compassion and selflessness as she dedicated her life to aiding India's impoverished individuals. She was a true embodiment of Virgos nurturing and service oriented traits.

- **Leo Tolstoy** (September 9 1828); Leo Tolstoy was an author and philosopher famous for his monumental work "War and Peace." He exemplified Virgos intellectual characteristics through his writings

As we come to the end of this chapter we can't help but be amazed by the stories, legends and historical events that revolve around the Virgo constellation. From Babylonians' deep respect for the goddess Shala. To the Greeks connections with Demeter and the Egyptians association with Isis. Virgo has symbolized fertility, agriculture and the nurturing forces of the universe. Its presence during the transition from summer to fall marked by the equinox further emphasizes its impact on human culture. In modern astrology Virgo continues to hold a radiant place as a sign, with an enduring legacy.

For readers who wish to delve deeper into the history and mythology of Virgo, here are some recommended primary sources, ancient texts, and modern writings:

- **"Star Names: Their Lore and Meaning"** by Richard H. Allen: This classic work provides insights into the origins and symbolism of constellations, including Virgo.
- **"The Secret Teachings of All Ages"** by Manly P. Hall: An esoteric exploration of ancient wisdom, including astrological symbolism and mythology.
- **"Mythology"** by Edith Hamilton: A comprehensive overview of Greek and Roman mythology, which includes the stories of Demeter, Isis, and other deities linked to Virgo.
- **"The Inner Sky"** by Steven Forrest: This modern astrology book explores the psychological dimensions of Virgo and other signs, offering insights into self-discovery and personal growth.

- **Online Resources:** Websites like the American Federation of Astrologers (AFA) and the Astrological Association of Great Britain provide valuable information on astrology's history, symbolism, and contemporary interpretations.

CHAPTER 2:
LOVE & COMPATIBILITY

When it comes to love and relationships Virgo individuals bring a combination of practicality, dedication and attention to detail. In this chapter we will explore how Virgo approaches matters of the heart and their compatibility, with other zodiac signs. This exploration will shed light on both the challenges and harmonious connections that arise when a Virgo meets someone from another star sign.

Whether you're a Virgo seeking insights into your tendencies or simply curious about building a fulfilling relationship with a Virgo, this chapter offers valuable guidance. Join us on this journey as we explore the secrets behind how Virgos approach matters of love.

THE VIRGO APPROACH TO LOVE

Virgo, being an Earth sign governed by Mercury approaches love in a way that combines practicality, analytical thinking and devotion. When Virgos experience love they do so with sincerity. Let's look closer at how Virgos approach love.

- **Analytical and Thoughtful**; Virgos are known for their analytical minds. In matters of the heart they take their time to carefully assess partners and relationships.
- **Attention to Detail**; Virgo's meticulous nature extends to their relationships. They pay close attention to the details, making considerate gestures and remembering important dates. This can make their partners feel cherished.
- **Practicality**; Virgos highly value stability and practicality. In matters of love, they often seek partners who share their life values. Dramatic or tumultuous relationships generally don't pique their interest. Instead they prefer a dependable partnership.
- **Loyalty and Dedication**; Once Virgos commit to a relationship they display loyalty and dedication. They are willing to put in the effort to

make the relationship thrive while standing by their partner through thick and thin.

- **Affectionate**; Virgos have an inclination to care for their loved ones. They show their affection by offering help organizing things and providing assistance whenever needed.

- **Sincere**; In matters of love Virgos tend to be humble and unpretentious. While they may not be the most romantic sign their love is genuine and unwavering.

- **Honesty**; Open and honest communication holds importance for Virgos in relationships. They value discussing issues, finding solutions and working together with their partners to establish a healthy connection.

- **Alone time**; Despite being committed partners Virgos also appreciate having space for themselves. They understand the significance of maintaining a sense of independence while nurturing the relationship.

- **Critical**; Due to their analytical nature Virgos can sometimes become excessively critical. Both towards themselves and their partners. Overall it would benefit them to learn how to balance this tendency in order to avoid conflicts.

- **Trust**; Trust is of huge importance for Virgos in a relationship. They need to feel secure and confident about their partners' loyalty.

To sum it up when it comes to love and romance Virgos tend to be practical, loyal and focused on building meaningful relationships. Virgos desire a balanced love life that allows both individuals to grow and flourish together.

They may not be extravagant in expressing their love but their commitment to the little things make them dependable partners.

COMPATIBILITY WITH OTHER SIGNS

VIRGO AND ARIES

Virgo and Aries are signs with distinct differences in their personalities and approaches to life. Virgo is practical, detail-oriented and prefers a structured routine. Aries, on the other hand, thrives on spontaneity. While they may be attracted to each other's strengths. For example, Aries' energy and Virgo's attention to detail, their differences can create challenges. Virgo may find Aries too impulsive and impatient. Aries may perceive Virgo as overly critical. For this pairing to work, they need to appreciate each other's unique qualities and find a balance.

VIRGO AND TAURUS

Virgo and Taurus share the Earth element, which grounds them and fosters stability. Both signs appreciate the finer things in life and value security and practicality. This is a highly compatible match. Virgo and Taurus understand each other's need for stability and are both dependable and loyal partners. They share common values. Overall they can build a strong and enduring relationship based on trust and shared goals.

VIRGO AND GEMINI

Virgo is practical and detail-oriented. Gemini is curious and adaptable. Gemini thrives on variety and intellectual stimulation. Both have contrasting approaches to life and may find it challenging to connect deeply. Virgo may see Gemini as flighty. Gemini may view Virgo as too serious. However, if they can communicate openly and appreciate each other's strengths, they can learn from each other. Overall they can then create a balanced relationship.

VIRGO AND CANCER

Both Virgo and Cancer are nurturing signs, albeit in different ways. Virgo nurtures through practical support. Cancer is emotionally nurturing. Together they can create a loving and supportive partnership. They share a deep emotional connection and understand each other's need for security. Virgo's practicality can complement Cancer's emotional sensitivity, creating a harmonious relationship.

VIRGO AND LEO

Virgo and Leo have contrasting personalities. Virgo is modest, detail-oriented and practical. Leo is confident, outgoing and seeks the spotlight. This pairing can be challenging due to their differences. Virgo may find Leo's need for attention overwhelming. Leo may perceive Virgo as overly critical. However, with effort and understanding, they can complement each other. Virgo's attention to detail can help Leo in their endeavors. Meanwhile Leo's charisma can bring excitement to Virgo's life.

VIRGO AND VIRGO

When two Virgos come together, they share a deep understanding of each other's tendencies. Positive and negative. Both value practicality and attention to detail. This can be a harmonious relationship based on shared values and a strong sense of responsibility. However, they may also share the tendency to be overly critical. It's essential for them to focus on mutual support and avoid nitpicking each other.

VIRGO AND LIBRA

Virgo and Libra have different approaches to life. Virgo is practical and detail-oriented. Libra is diplomatic and values harmony. This pairing can be challenging, as their priorities differ. Virgo may find Libra's indecisiveness frustrating. Meanwhile Libra might see Virgo as overly critical. To make it work, they need to appreciate each other's strengths. Together they can find ways to balance their differences.

VIRGO AND SCORPIO

Both Virgo and Scorpio are analytical and value deep emotional connections. They share a mutual dedication to their goals. This pairing can create a strong and passionate bond. They understand each other's intensity and need for privacy. Virgo's practicality can complement Scorpio's emotional depth, making them a well-rounded couple.

VIRGO AND SAGITTARIUS

Virgo is practical and detail-oriented. Sagittarius is adventurous and loves spontaneity and freedom. This pair can face challenges due to their differing priorities. Virgo may feel that Sagittarius is too carefree, while Sagittarius might perceive Virgo as too serious. For this relationship to work, they need to respect each other's need for both structure and spontaneity.

VIRGO AND CAPRICORN

Virgo and Capricorn are both Earth signs. This means they share common values such as stability and practicality. This is a highly compatible match. Virgo and Capricorn understand each other's goals and ambitions. As such they support each other's efforts. Together they can build a stable and prosperous life together. One based on mutual trust and shared values.

VIRGO AND AQUARIUS

Virgo is practical and detail-oriented. Aquarius is independent and values innovation and freedom. This pair may have challenges due to their differing priorities. Virgo may find Aquarius too unpredictable. Aquarius might perceive Virgo as too structured. To make it work, they need to find a balance between Virgo's practicality and Aquarius' need for freedom.

VIRGO AND PISCES

Virgo and Pisces have different approaches to life. Virgo is practical and analytical. Pisces is intuitive and emotionally sensitive. This can be a complementary match, as they balance each other's strengths and weaknesses. Virgo's practicality can provide stability to Pisces. Meanwhile Pisces' emotional depth can help Virgo connect on a more profound level. However, Virgo may need to be careful not to be overly critical of Pisces' sensitive nature.

TIPS FOR RELATIONSHIPS WITH VIRGO INDIVIDUALS

Dating and being in a relationship with a Virgo can be truly fulfilling. They are known for their loyalty and practical nature. To establish a better connection with a Virgo partner here are some tailored tips.

TIPS FOR MEN DATING VIRGO WOMEN

- **Respect Her Independence**; Virgo women highly value their independence and personal space. It's important to respect her need for alone time. In addition, encourage her to pursue her interests and goals.

- **Be Thoughtful**; Pay attention to the details. Virgo women appreciate romantic gestures. Remember important dates. Surprise her with small gifts or lend a hand with practical tasks when needed.

- **Engage in Intellectual Conversations**; Virgo women often have an interest in intellectual topics. Engage in such conversations. Share your ideas and be open to discussing subjects of her interest.

- **Be Patient and Supportive**; Virgo women can be self critical and strive for perfection. Offer support and reassurance when she doubts herself. Be patient as she pursues excellence.

- **Maintain Cleanliness**; Virgo women appreciate cleanliness and organization. By keeping your living spaces neat and tidy she will feel more comfortable and relaxed.

TIPS FOR WOMEN DATING VIRGO MEN

- **Appreciate His Practicality**; Virgo men are known for being individuals who can be relied upon. Express your gratitude, for his problem solving skills and their dedication to making your life easier.

- **Openness**; It's important to be open in your communication with Virgo men. Share your thoughts and feelings honestly so that they can better understand your needs and desires.

- **Support their passions**; Support their hobbies or interests. Whatever it is. Whether it's a passion for fitness, a love for books or a fascination with technology.

- **Patience**; Remember to be patient when faced with criticism from Virgo men. For them they often intend it to be feedback aimed at helping you improve.
- **Problem solving;** When planning dates consider activities that involve problem solving or learning something. For example cooking classes, DIY projects or visits to museums and exhibits.

Overall when dating a Virgo it's important to prioritize loyalty, honesty and reliability. Both partners should also strive for a balance between practicality (a characteristic often associated with Virgos) and the need for spontaneity within the relationship.

In our exploration of love and compatibility, within the Virgo zodiac sign we have delved into the essence of this grounded and practical sign. Virgos possess an approach to love and relationships combining their minds with their nurturing spirits. Throughout this chapter we have revealed the intricacies of Virgos tendencies. We have explored how they connect with each of the twelve zodiac signs. From forming enduring partnerships with Taurus to experiencing synergy with Capricorn. Overall we have uncovered the potential for love and connection that Virgo shares with every star sign.

As we conclude this chapter it is important to understand that while astrology offers insights, it is ultimately the blend of personalities, experiences and choices that shape our romantic connections. The compatibility guidelines presented here serve as a starting point. Ultimately love goes beyond zodiac boundaries. By embracing effective communication we can cultivate lasting and rewarding relationships not only with Virgos but also with people, from all walks of life.

CHAPTER 3:
FRIENDS AND FAMILY

In this chapter we will uncover the subtleties of how Virgos approach family bonds and friendships. We will highlight both the strengths and the potential challenges they may encounter. Whether you're a Virgo seeking an understanding of your role in your loved ones lives, or someone to appreciate the unique qualities that Virgo friends and family members possess. This chapter will provide valuable insights. Join us as we explore the dynamics of familial ties, for Virgos and the enduring connections forged in the realm of friendship.

When you have a friend who's a Virgo, you can count on having a reliable companion. One with a unique blend of qualities that enhance your friendship. Let's take a close look at what it's like to have a Virgo friend.

- **Reliability**; Having a Virgo friend means having a reliable person in your life. They are punctually organized and follow through on their commitments.
- **Attention to Detail**; Virgos possess an eye for detail. They have an ability to notice things that others may overlook. This makes them excellent problem solvers and planners.
- **Problem Solvers**; Virgo friends excel at analyzing complex situations and finding practical solutions. When faced with dilemmas they offer valuable insights.
- **Loyalty**; Above all else Virgos are fiercely loyal to their friends. They stand by your side through thick and thin.
- **Practical Support**; Virgo friends are always ready to assist you whether it's helping, with your move, organizing an event or providing advice.
- **Modesty**; Virgo individuals have a modest nature. They prefer to work behind the scenes rather than seeking attention. As such they find joy in supporting their friends' endeavors.
- **Honesty**; Honesty and integrity hold value for Virgo friends. They offer feedback with the intention of aiding your growth and improvement.

- **Analytical Listening**; When you share your thoughts and concerns with a Virgo friend they listen attentively. In turn they excel at providing feedback from perspectives you might have overlooked. They want you to succeed so they provide guidance considerately.
- **Tidiness**; Virgo friends appreciate cleanliness and orderliness. Spending time with them often means enjoying organized spaces and environments. However it's important to note that due to their pursuit of perfection, Virgos may sometimes become overly critical of themselves or others. They might also tend to worry a lot. As a friend it's important to provide reassurance and remind them to take it easy when necessary.

To sum up, having a Virgo friend means having someone who's loyal, practical and pays attention to details. Their distinctive qualities enrich the strength and depth of your friendship making it a bond worth treasuring. Ultimately they will always be there for you.

VIRGO AND FAMILY DYNAMICS

Virgo individuals, bring a combination of practicality skills and dedication to their families. When they actively engage in family life they do so with a sense of responsibility and a genuine desire to nurture and support their loved ones. Now let's take a closer look at how Virgos contribute to the dynamics within the family.

- **Nurturing**; Virgos possess an ability to nurture others. They take their caregiver roles seriously.

As such they are always ready to offer support
and practical assistance to their family.

- **Attention to Detail**; Known for their
  meticulousness Virgos excel in organizing and
  planning. Their attention to detail becomes an
  asset within the context of family life.

- **Reliability**; If you have a Virgo as a part of your
  family you can rely on them without hesitation.
  They are known for being individuals who will go
  above and beyond to fulfill their responsibilities.

- **Problem Solvers**; Thanks to their analytical
  nature Virgos make excellent problem solvers
  within the family. Whenever conflicts or
  challenges arise they often step up as mediators
  who propose solutions.

- **Health**; Virgos prioritize healthy living for
  themselves as well as for those around them.
  They often show an interest in the well being of
  their family members. As such they are usually
  encouraging health habits and providing support
  during times of illness.

- **Modest**; When it comes to family interactions
  Virgos tend to be modest and unassuming. They
  prefer to work behind the scenes rather than
  seeking the spotlight.

- **Honesty**; Open and honest communication is
  highly valued by Virgos within their families.
  They are willing to discuss any issues or conflicts
  that arise in order to find solutions and promote
  harmony at home.

- **Routine**; Virgos appreciate having a routine and
  structure in their lives. They may play a role in
  establishing and maintaining household

schedules. Overall this can bring stability and a sense of security for everyone involved.

- **Mentor**; In the family dynamic Virgo members often take on the role of teacher or mentor. They derive joy from sharing their knowledge and skills with loved ones while taking pride in helping them learn and grow.
- **Listeners**; While they may not always openly express their emotions Virgos excel at listening. Family members can rely on them for providing a space where they can share their feelings and concerns receiving advice along with comfort.

To sum up, Virgos make valuable contributions to family dynamics due to their caring supportive traits. They play key roles in ensuring the well being of the family. In times of conflicts or challenges they are there mediating or offering practical assistance. As a result they are seen as cherished members of the family.

CHALLENGES IN FRIENDSHIPS AND FAMILY RELATIONS FOR VIRGO

While Virgos possess positive qualities in their friendships and family relationships they also face certain unique challenges. It's crucial to acknowledge these pitfalls in order to cultivate harmonious connections with individuals who are Virgos. Let's explore how.

- **Being Overly Critical**; Virgos are renowned for their attention to detail and relentless pursuit of perfection. However this characteristic can sometimes make them excessively critical of themselves as others. Within friendships and family dynamics this tendency to be overly judgmental can become burdensome for those who feel constantly evaluated or scrutinized.

- **Worry**; Virgos have a tendency to be worriers by nature. They may find themselves constantly preoccupied with the well being of their loved ones. If not properly managed this anxiety can introduce tension into relationships.

- **Difficulty Expressing Emotions**; Virgos often feel more at ease expressing gestures or offering solutions than articulating their emotions verbally. This inclination can pose a challenge for friends and family members who strive to comprehend their sentiments or needs accurately.

- **Perfectionism**; The desire for perfection that characterizes Virgos can result in high expectations for both themselves and those around them. Consequently this may create an environment of pressure and stress within relationships where others feel compelled to meet high standards.

- **Self Criticism**; It is worth noting that Virgos tend to be especially hard on themselves when it comes to self evaluation. This tendency to criticize themselves can affect their relationships when they impose their standards on others.

- **Concern for Health**; Virgos are individuals who prioritize health and may sometimes worry excessively about the well being of their loved ones. While it's natural to be concerned, excessive worry can create stress in relationships.

- **Preference for Structure**; Virgos can be inflexible at times preferring routines and structure. This preference for predictability may clash with the spontaneity or adaptability of friends or family members.

- **Introverted Nature;** Some Virgos lean towards introversion which means they may require more time compared to extroverted friends or family members. Also their need for solitude can sometimes be misinterpreted as a lack of interest or emotional distance.

- **Difficulty Seeking Help**; Virgos often prefer being the ones offering assistance and support rather than receiving it. This inclination might make it challenging for friends and family to offer help when it's needed.

As we come to the end of this chapter let's reflect on what we have discovered. Virgos bring a combination of qualities to their relationships with family and friends. They take care in nurturing their families paying attention to the smallest details. They offer solutions when faced with problems and show unwavering loyalty to their companions. Their presence adds depth and richness to our connections, with others making their contributions truly invaluable.

As we conclude this chapter, we celebrate the unique role Virgo individuals play in their families and friendships. Their dedication, practicality and unwavering support are invaluable assets. Ones that enrich the lives of those fortunate enough to have them in their circle. Through open communication, mutual understanding and a willingness to embrace both strengths and weaknesses, the bonds with Virgo friends and family members can flourish. As a result these relationships will continue to be a source of enduring love and support.

CHAPTER 4: CAREER AND MONEY

In this chapter we will delve into the world of how Virgos approach their lives and their relationship with money. When it comes to careers and finances, Virgos bring a powerful combination of practicality, attention to detail and a strong work ethic.

Throughout this chapter we will explore in detail the strengths and challenges that Virgo individuals face in their careers and financial journeys. Whether you're a Virgo seeking insights into your path or someone about how Virgos handle money matters this chapter will provide valuable guidance.

VIRGO CAREER PREFERENCES AND PROFESSIONAL ASPIRATIONS

As mentioned above, Virgos bring a powerful combination of practicality, attention to detail and a strong work ethic to their lives. Their meticulous nature and desire for order make them well suited for certain career paths. Here's an overview of Virgos career preferences and aspirations.

- **Precision and Attention to Detail;** Virgos excel in careers that demand precision and meticulousness. They have a unique ability to identify errors and inconsistencies. This makes them valuable in various fields. For example auditing, quality control, data analysis and accounting.
- **Service Oriented Professions;** Many Virgos are inclined towards careers that involve helping others. They thrive in roles such as healthcare professionals (nurses, doctors, pharmacists) social work, counseling and teaching.
- **Administrative and Organizational Roles;** Virgos are often sought after for positions that require task management, scheduling expertise and resource coordination. These roles can

include assistants, project managers, event planners and office managers.

- **Research & Analysis**; Virgos possess analytical skills and a talent for research. They have the potential to thrive in paths, such as those of scientists, researchers, analysts and statisticians. These careers highly appreciate their skills in collecting and analyzing data.

- **Writing and Editing**; Virgos possess a talent for writing, editing and proofreading tasks. Their meticulousness when it comes to language usage and grammar makes them exceptional editors, content creators and technical writers.

- **Wellness**; Due to their healthy nature Virgos are often drawn towards healthcare and wellness professions. They may choose careers as dietitians, nutritionists, physical therapists or alternative healthcare practitioners.

- **Agricultural Fields**; With their connection to the Earth element Virgos find themselves well suited for careers related to the environment and agriculture. They may flourish as scientists, farmers or horticulturists.

- **Consulting**; The analytical abilities of Virgos make them highly valuable in consulting roles where problem solving skills are crucial. They excel at providing solutions and recommendations in areas like management consulting IT consulting or financial advisory services.

- **Entrepreneurship**; Virgos attention to detail and strong work ethic are great traits for entrepreneurs. They might focus on areas such as e-commerce platforms, small scale manufacturing or service oriented startups.

- **Education and Training;** Virgos often derive satisfaction from roles related to education and training. They excel as teachers, mentors and trainers who can patiently and precisely guide others.

- **Philanthropy;** Virgos are frequently driven by a sense of serving others. They may pursue careers in charity organizations where they can have a meaningful impact.

- **Holistic and Wellness Practices;** Virgos naturally have an interest in well being. Some might explore careers in areas such as health, yoga instruction or holistic therapy aligning their work with their values.

STRENGTHS THAT MAKE VIRGO INDIVIDUALS EXCEL IN THE WORKPLACE

Virgo individuals possess a set of qualities that make them exceptional in the workplace. Here are some of the strengths that distinguish Virgo. One should focus on building on these.

- **Attention to Detail;** Virgos possess an ability to observe the smallest details. This keen eye allows them to identify errors, inconsistencies and find opportunities for improvement that others may overlook.

- **Strong Work Ethic;** Virgo individuals are renowned for their diligence. They take their responsibilities seriously. Their dedication makes them reliable and trustworthy members of any team.

- **Organizational Skills;** Virgos flourish in structured environments. They have a talent for organizing tasks, schedules and projects effectively.
- **Analytical Thinking;** Virgos excel at problem solving and analysis. They have a knack for breaking down issues and finding practical solutions. Overall these strengths make Virgo individuals highly effective professionals, across various industries.
- **Flexibility;** Although Virgos are known for their inclination towards structure they also possess the ability to adapt.
- **Effective Communication;** Virgos excel in articulate communication both in written form and verbally. Their attention to detail extends to conveying ideas and information. This skill proves advantageous in professions that prioritize communication, such as teaching, writing or customer service.
- **Dependability;** Virgos strong sense of responsibility and dedication towards their work makes them highly reliable employees. They consistently follow through on their commitments ensuring delivery of results.
- **Team Player Mentality;** Virgo thrive as team players who collaborate effectively with others. They readily embrace collaboration opportunities while often taking on roles within teams. Their positive contribution to group efforts fosters a positive work environment.

- **Excelling in Time Management**; Virgos possess high level skills in managing their time. They prioritize tasks, set deadlines and maintain a professional approach to their work. This ability to manage time effectively greatly contributes to their productivity.

- **Embracing Growth;** Virgos are always on the lookout for ways to improve themselves and their work. They welcome feedback and seek opportunities for learning and development. This helps them stay current and competitive in their careers.

The above strengths collectively make Virgo valuable assets in any workplace. Next let's look at some of the challenges they may face.

CHALLENGES FACED BY VIRGO IN THEIR CAREERS AND STRATEGIES TO OVERCOME THEM

Virgo individuals despite their strengths may face challenges in their professional lives. Being aware of these challenges and implementing strategies to overcome them can help them navigate their careers successfully. Here are some common difficulties that Virgos often encounter in the workplace, along with strategies to overcome them.

Perfectionism

- Challenge; Virgos are known for their pursuit of perfection which can sometimes lead to setting unrealistic expectations for themselves and others.

- Strategy; It is important for Virgos to practice self compassion and understand that perfection is an ideal that may not always be attainable. Setting goals and recognizing that mistakes provide opportunities for growth can be helpful.

Being Overly Critical

- Challenge; Because of their attention to detail Virgos may tend to be overly critical at times. As such it could strain relationships with colleagues.
- Strategy; When providing feedback or constructive criticism it is advisable for Virgos to focus on being constructive. Recognizing the efforts of others and emphasizing solutions of dwelling on problems can foster relationships.

Worry and Anxiety

- Challenge; Virgos sometimes experience worry and anxiety about their performance. Ultimately this can lead to stress and potential burnout.
- Strategy; Developing stress management techniques like mindfulness practices can be beneficial for managing worry and anxiety. Additionally seeking support could also aid in managing these feelings.

Difficulty Delegating

- Challenge; Virgos often find it hard to entrust tasks to others as they strive for excellence. This can result in a heavy workload.

- Strategy; It is important for Virgos to learn the art of delegation. By placing trust in colleagues and subordinates they can lighten their load.

Overload of Details

- Challenge; Virgos may feel overwhelmed, by the abundance of details they need to manage which can impede productivity.
- Strategy; To overcome this challenge Virgos should develop work systems. Utilizing technology tools for task management and prioritizing tasks based on their importance and urgency will help them stay on track.

Self Criticism

- Challenge; Virgos tend to be extremely self critical often struggling with issues related to self esteem.
- Strategy; Cultivating self compassion is crucial for overcoming this challenge. Engaging in positive self talk and taking time to acknowledge achievements are essential steps.

Resistance to Change

- Challenge; Virgos may exhibit resistance towards change.
- Strategy; Embrace change as an avenue for growth and learning. Staying updated on industry trends and technological advancements will allow Virgos to remain competitive and adaptive.

Difficulty Expressing Emotions

- Challenge; Virgos sometimes encounter difficulty in expressing their emotions which can hinder communication.
- Strategy; It's important to engage in honest communication with your colleagues. Express your thoughts and emotions when necessary in team settings or when resolving conflicts.

Reluctance to Seek Help

- Challenge; Virgos often prefer being the ones offering help rather than seeking assistance themselves which can lead to burnout.
- Strategy; Recognize that asking for help is a sign of strength, not weakness. When you need support don't hesitate to seek guidance or delegate tasks as it helps maintain a work life balance.

Balancing Work and Personal Life

- Challenge; Virgos strong work ethic may cause them to prioritize their careers over their personal lives.
- Strategy; Set boundaries between work and personal life. Make self care hobbies and spending time with loved ones a priority in order to maintain a work life balance.

As we wrap up this chapter it is clear that Virgos accomplishments in their careers and financial stability are a testament to their commitment to hard work. Their skill in navigating the complexities of work and wealth management is an asset that enriches not only their own lives but also the lives of those around them.

However, like everyone, Virgos face challenges such as striving for perfectionism and being overly critical of themselves. These challenges can be seen as opportunities for growth when acknowledged and addressed. May these insights give you the strength and clarity to navigate your journey, towards success and financial security while aligning with the order of the universe.

CHAPTER 5:
SELF-IMPROVEMENT

In this chapter we set sail on an exploration, through the realm of self improvement. We are about to traverse the cosmos uncovering how Virgo individuals can utilize their qualities to become the versions of themselves. From their mindset and analytical thinking to their inclination towards perfectionism and critical nature. Virgos face unique advantages and challenges that shape their personal growth journey.

Join us as we delve into the choreography of self improvement, where Virgos strive relentlessly to become the best versions of themselves.

PERSONAL GROWTH AND DEVELOPMENT FOR VIRGO

People born under the zodiac sign of Virgo, possess a powerful set of qualities that can contribute to growth and development. That is when nurtured effectively. Here are some important aspects of growth for individuals with a Virgo zodiac sign.

- **Embrace Self Compassion**; Virgos often hold themselves to high standards. This can sometimes lead to self criticism and striving for perfection. Understand that making mistakes is acceptable. Ultimately one's self worth isn't solely determined by their achievements.
- **Find Balance in Attention to Detail;** While being detail oriented is a positive trait it's essential not to become overly consumed by the details. Virgos can experience growth by learning when to focus on specifics and when it's necessary to step back.
- **Explore Emotional Expression**; Virgos tend to approach life from a logical standpoint. They may find it challenging to express their emotions openly. Personal growth involves developing the ability to connect with emotions for improved relationships and self awareness.
- **Manage Worry and Anxiety**; It is common for Virgos to experience worry and anxiety.

Practicing mindfulness, meditation or stress reduction techniques can greatly contribute to mental health.

- **Being adaptable**; While Virgos tend to appreciate routine and structure, personal growth often involves embracing change and being adaptable. Learning to be more flexible and open to experiences is key for development.

- **Listen intently**; Virgos are known for their precise communication skills, which's a strength. However personal growth can also involve improving listening skills.

- **Stepping out of the comfort zone**; Virgos have a tendency to avoid taking risks. Personal development however, often requires taking risks and stepping out of comfort zones. Embrace opportunities for growth and learning.

- **Set boundaries**; Virgos strong work ethic may sometimes lead them to overwork or neglecting their personal lives. Set boundaries, prioritize self care and find a work life balance.

- **Education**; Virgos love for knowledge and learning is an asset for growth. Continuously pursuing skills, hobbies or further education can lead to more personal development.

- **Seek Support and Feedback**; Although Virgos tend to prefer handling challenges themselves, seeking support can accelerate growth

To pursue growth and development effectively Virgos can tap into their qualities while embracing flexibility and self compassion. By maintaining a balance between their strengths and areas where they can grow further, Virgo individuals can evolve into more successful individuals.

HARNESSING STRENGTHS AND OVERCOMING WEAKNESSES

To lead fulfilling lives and unleash their fullest potential Virgos can utilize their qualities while also working on overcoming challenges. Here's a helpful guide on how to achieve that.

- **Attention to Detail (Strength);** Utilize your precise nature in roles that demand precision, such as data analysis, quality control or project management. To avoid hindering progress it's important not to get too caught up in details. Learn how to effectively prioritize tasks.

- **Strong Work Ethic (Strength);** Fully commit yourself to tasks and projects with the delivery of high quality results. However it's crucial to also keep an eye on maintaining a work life balance. Never neglect your well being.
- **Practicality (Strength);** Leverage your analytical mindset for solving real world problems and making decisions. At the same time make sure not to let practicality stifle creativity. Allow space for imaginative thinking.
- **Organization Skills (Strength);** Effectively manage schedules, tasks and resources to bring order out of chaos. Nevertheless avoid becoming too rigid in your approach. Embrace adaptability when planning.
- **Communication Skills (Strength);** Embrace the ability to express your thoughts and ideas clearly. This will help you to effectively communicate in many situations. To overcome any challenges, focus on listening to others. Understand other perspectives and build connections.
- **Analytical Thinking (Strength);** Leverage your skills to break down problems and offer practical solutions. Avoid getting caught up in overanalyzing situations as it can lead to indecisiveness. Trust your instincts when necessary.
- **Perfectionism (Weakness);** Striving for perfection is a great attitude. However it can be unrealistic. Recognize that making mistakes is a part of growth and development. Shift your focus from being overly critical, towards embracing

criticism. Prioritize finding solutions rather than dwelling on problems.

- **Worry and Anxiety (Weakness);** Develop stress management techniques like mindfulness or meditation to reduce worry and anxiety.
- **Difficulty Expressing Emotions (Weakness);** Work on expressing your feelings particularly within personal relationships. Practice communicating emotions with authenticity.
- **Reluctance to Seek Help (Weakness);** Understand that seeking assistance is a sign of strength rather than weakness. Embrace the opportunity for growth by reaching out for support when needed.
- **Resistance to Change (Weakness);** View change as an avenue, for growth and learning. Embrace new opportunities instead of resisting them.
- **Self Criticism (Weakness);** To overcome self criticism it's essential to cultivate self compassion. Take the time to celebrate your achievements and recognize your worth, beyond accomplishments.
- **Balancing Work and Personal Life (Weakness);** Establishing boundaries between work and personal life is crucial. Prioritize self care. Make sure to spend quality time with loved ones.

By acknowledging strengths and actively addressing weaknesses Virgos can lead successful lives. As Virgos progress, on their journey of self improvement they not only become the finest versions of themselves but also serve as inspiring mentors.

In conclusion, this chapter has shed light on the path that Virgos tread, characterized by a focus on practicality, attention to detail and a constant drive towards reaching their potential. May this understanding ignite a renewed sense of enthusiasm and determination in Virgos. In addition may it also add value to those accompanying them as they embark on their expedition, towards self improvement.

CHAPTER 6:
THE YEAR AHEAD

The stars and planets have long been our celestial guides, providing a roadmap to navigate the intricacies of life. For Virgo individuals, the year ahead holds the promise of growth, transformation and many opportunities. While astrology doesn't dictate destiny, it does offer valuable insights.

Throughout this chapter, we'll delve into the influences of key astrological events, highlighting significant dates and time periods that hold particular importance. From the impact on love and relationships to career prospects, health, the potential for personal growth and much more.

Whether you are a Virgo seeking insights to make the most of the year ahead or someone interested in understanding how the stars align for Virgo. This chapter provides a celestial compass to navigate the cosmic currents that will shape the year ahead. Join us as we explore the cosmic dance of Virgo in the year ahead!

HOROSCOPE GUIDE FOR VIRGO INDIVIDUALS

The year ahead holds promise and opportunities for Virgo individuals. With your innate practicality and attention to detail, you can make significant strides in various areas of your life. Here's a glimpse of what the stars may have in store for you in the coming year.

CAREER AND FINANCES

Your career prospects look positive this year. Your meticulous approach and analytical thinking will help you excel in your current role or to take on new challenges. Be open to innovative solutions. Don't hesitate to share your ideas with colleagues. Financially, your careful budgeting and saving habits will pay off.

Astrological events can provide insights into potential career growth and financial stability. Here's a closer look at how the year's astrological events may impact Virgo individuals' professional lives.

- **Mercury Retrogrades** (Dates: Multiple throughout the year): Mercury, the ruling planet of Virgo, will have its retrograde periods. These can affect communication and decision-making at work. Exercise caution in professional interactions and avoid signing contracts during these times.
- **Saturn Transits** (Throughout the year): Saturn's influence may bring lessons and challenges in your career. Embrace responsibilities and challenges with discipline, as they can lead to long-term growth and success.
- **New Moons in Virgo** (Dates: To be determined): New Moons in Virgo are opportunities for setting practical career goals and initiating projects that align with your ambitions.

Use this time to plan and focus on your professional growth.

- **Jupiter Transits** (Throughout the year): Jupiter's presence can expand your career horizons. Be open to new job opportunities, promotions, or collaborations. These may enhance your professional life and financial prospects.

LOVE AND RELATIONSHIPS

In matters of the heart, expect growth and deepening connections. For singles, there are chances to meet someone special through work or mutual interests. For those in relationships, open communication will strengthen your love. Be sure to balance your dedication to work with quality time for your loved ones. The stars favor harmony in your relationships this year.

Virgo individuals can anticipate a year influenced by astrological events that will impact their romantic lives. While the stars do not dictate destiny, they can offer guidance on potential opportunities and challenges. Here's a look at how astrological events in the upcoming year may influence Virgo individuals' love lives.

- **Venus in Virgo** (Date: August 16 to September 10): When Venus, the planet of love and harmony, enters Virgo, it can enhance Virgo individuals' romantic connections. This period offers an opportunity to strengthen existing relationships and express love.
- **New Moons in Virgo** (Dates: To be determined): New Moons signify new beginnings. When they occur in Virgo, they encourage Virgos

to set practical relationship goals. It's a time for introspection, self-improvement and initiating positive changes.

- **Jupiter Transits** (Throughout the year): Jupiter's influence can bring expansion and growth to your love life. Be open to new experiences and connections. Jupiter's positive energy may lead to romantic opportunities and personal growth within relationships.

- **Lunar Eclipses** (Dates: To be determined): Lunar eclipses can bring revelations and shifts in your emotional life. Embrace changes in your relationships. Overall they often pave the way for personal growth and positive transformation.

HEALTH AND WELL-BEING

Maintaining good health should always be a priority. Pay attention to your stress levels. Your natural tendency to worry can affect your well-being. Consider incorporating mindfulness practices. For example yoga or meditation. A balanced diet and regular exercise will further contribute to your overall vitality.

Astrological events can offer insights into how you can maintain your well-being. Here's a look at how the year's astrological events may affect Virgo individuals' health and wellness.

- **Lunar Eclipses** (Dates: To be determined): Lunar eclipses may signal the need for change in your daily routines and habits. Embrace these opportunities for self-improvement and prioritize self-care practices.

- **Venus in Virgo** (Date: August 16 to September 10): During this period, focus on self-love and self-care. Pamper yourself and engage in activities that promote emotional and physical well-being.
- **Mindfulness and Stress Management**: Given Virgo's tendency to worry, consider incorporating mindfulness, meditation, or stress-reduction techniques into your daily routine. These practices can help manage anxiety and promote overall health.

PERSONAL GROWTH AND SPIRITUALITY

The year ahead offers numerous opportunities for personal growth and self-discovery. Embrace change and step out of your comfort zone to explore new horizons. Pursue hobbies or interests that ignite your creativity and passion. Engaging in spiritual practices or self-reflection can provide valuable insights into your inner self. Astrological events can guide you on this journey of self-improvement. Here's how you can use these events to facilitate personal growth.

- **New Moons in Virgo** (Dates: To be determined): Utilize New Moons in Virgo as moments of introspection and goal-setting. Set intentions for self-improvement. Take practical steps toward personal growth.
- **Jupiter Transits** (Throughout the year): Embrace new experiences and opportunities for growth. Jupiter's positive influence can expand your horizons and lead to personal development in various aspects of your life.
- **Lunar Eclipses** (Dates: To be determined): Welcome changes and transformations, even if they initially feel challenging. Lunar eclipses often signify moments of growth and self-discovery.

FAMILY AND HOME LIFE

Family relationships will be a source of support and joy this year. Plan quality time with loved ones to nurture these bonds. If you've been considering home-related changes, such as redecorating or moving, this could be a perfect time.

TRAVEL AND ADVENTURE

If travel is on your mind, the stars encourage exploration and adventure. Whether it's a short getaway or a more extended journey. Truly, you'll find inspiration and personal growth through new experiences. Embrace spontaneity and relish the unexpected.

SOCIAL LIFE

Your social circle may expand this year. Networking could lead to exciting opportunities. Attend social events, join clubs, or participate in group activities to broaden your connections. Your practical advice and problem-solving abilities will make you a valuable member of any community.

Ultimately as a Virgo individual, you have the potential to make the most of the year ahead. Do this by being proactive in your love life, career, health and personal growth. The stars offer guidance, but it's your actions and choices that will ultimately shape your journey in the coming year.

KEY ASTROLOGICAL EVENTS AND THEIR IMPACT ON VIRGO:

Astrological events can have a significant influence on the lives and experiences of individuals born under the Virgo sign. These celestial occurrences can shape various aspects of Virgos' lives, including their personal growth, relationships and career. Here are some key astrological events and their potential impact on Virgo individuals.

Mercury Retrogrades

- Impact: Mercury is the ruling planet of Virgo, and its retrogrades may affect communication and decision-making.
- Advice: During Mercury retrogrades, be extra cautious with contracts, communication and travel plans. Take time to review and revise and practice patience in all interactions.

New Moons in Virgo

- Impact: New Moons signify new beginnings, and when they occur in Virgo, it's a time for setting practical goals and initiating projects.
- Advice: Use New Moons in Virgo as opportunities to make plans, set intentions and focus on self-improvement.

Full Moons in Pisces (Opposite Sign)

- Impact: Full Moons in Pisces, the opposite sign of Virgo, can bring emotional intensity and challenges.
- Advice: Be mindful of heightened emotions during these periods. Balance your practicality with empathy and self-care.

Jupiter Transits

- Impact: When Jupiter, the planet of expansion and growth, transits through Virgo or compatible signs, it can bring opportunities. Both for personal and professional development.
- Advice: Embrace new opportunities and take calculated risks. Explore areas of personal growth during Jupiter transits.

Saturn Transits

- Impact: Saturn transits can bring lessons and challenges, pushing Virgos to mature and take on greater responsibilities.
- Advice: Face challenges with determination and discipline. Saturn's influence can lead to long-term growth and success.

Venus in Virgo

- Impact: When Venus, the planet of love and harmony, enters Virgo, it can enhance Virgo individuals' relationships.

- Advice: Use this time to nurture existing relationships and engage in acts of self-love and self-care.

Solar Eclipses

- Impact: Solar eclipses can bring significant changes and new beginnings. Their influence varies depending on the eclipse's position in the zodiac.
- Advice: Pay attention to eclipses in compatible signs, as they may signal opportunities for growth and transformation.

Lunar Eclipses

- Impact: Lunar eclipses can signal the culmination of projects or relationships, bringing closure and revelations.
- Advice: Embrace the changes that lunar eclipses bring, even if they initially feel challenging. They often pave the way for positive transformations.

Ultimately it's important to remember that astrological events provide a framework for understanding cosmic energies. However individual experiences may vary. While astrology provides a compass it is ultimately the choices we make as Virgos that shape our destiny. Virgo individuals can use astrology as a tool for self-awareness and personal growth. They can make the most of favorable influences and navigate challenges with wisdom.

Reflecting upon these insights we can gather guidance for Virgo individuals as they navigate the year ahead. The alignment of stars and planets has created a tapestry of influences that bring forth both opportunities and challenges in love, relationships, career, finances, health, wellness, personal growth and self discovery. Throughout this year's journey it is important for Virgo individuals to embrace change willingly while nurturing their relationships. Prioritizing self care and actively pursuing growth with determination will also prove to be beneficial.

The celestial events highlighted in this chapter provide moments for reflection, setting goals and experiencing transformation. May the year ahead be filled with love, success, good health and personal growth. The universe provides its guidance. In the end it's up to you to navigate your journey. Take the opportunity for a rewarding and purposeful year. A great one is within your reach!

CHAPTER 7:
FAMOUS "VIRGO" PERSONALITIES

Virgos are widely recognized for their attention to detail, unwavering work ethic and their relentless pursuit of perfection. In this chapter we embark on a journey exploring the lives and accomplishments of famous people born under the zodiac of Virgo. As we delve into these profiles you will discover the Virgo qualities and traits that define them. From musicians and legendary actors, to leaders and celebrated authors, Virgos have made lasting impressions in many domains.

Join us on this tour as we delve into their lives, careers and contributions. Lets celebrate their dedication, precision driven approach and tireless pursuit of excellence. Their stories stand as a testament to the potential possessed by those born under the sign of Virgo. Furthermore they provide inspiration for all who aspire to excel in their chosen paths.

MICHAEL JACKSON

- Date of Birth: August 29, 1958.
- Brief Biography: Michael Jackson, often referred to as the "King of Pop," was a legendary American singer, songwriter and dancer. He rose to fame as a member of the Jackson 5. Later he enjoyed a highly successful solo career. His

groundbreaking albums, including "Thriller," remain some of the best-selling in music history.

- Virgo Traits: Meticulous attention to detail, strong work ethic and dedication to his craft.

- Impact: Michael Jackson's influence on the music industry is immeasurable. He revolutionized pop music, set new standards for music videos and left an enduring legacy. His philanthropic efforts also left a significant impact on humanitarian causes.

- Personal Life: Despite his worldwide fame, Jackson was known for his private and enigmatic persona. He faced numerous controversies and legal challenges throughout his life. Jackson's untimely death in 2009 marked the end of an era in music. He left behind a legacy that continues to inspire and entertain.

BARBARA BACH

- Date of Birth: August 27, 1947.
- Brief Biography: Barbara Bach is an American actress and model best known for her roles in the James Bond film "The Spy Who Loved Me" and the fantasy film "Caveman." She gained international recognition for her beauty and acting talent during the 1970s and 1980s.
- Virgo Traits: Attention to detail, strong work ethic and commitment to her career.
- Impact: Barbara Bach's presence in Hollywood during her prime left an indelible mark on the film industry. Her performances and beauty made her a prominent figure in the entertainment world.
- Personal Life: Barbara Bach's personal life includes her marriage to Ringo Starr, the drummer of The Beatles. She has also been involved in various charitable endeavors and continues to be a beloved figure in the entertainment industry.

KOBE BRYANT

- Date of Birth: August 23, 1978.
- Brief Biography: Kobe Bryant was an iconic American professional basketball player who

spent his entire 20-year career with the Los
Angeles Lakers in the NBA. He is regarded as
one of the greatest basketball players of all time,
winning numerous championships and accolades.

- Virgo Traits: Exceptional work ethic and
dedication to his sport.

- Impact: Kobe Bryant's impact on the game of
basketball and sports culture as a whole is
immense. He inspired countless athletes with his
competitive spirit, leadership and commitment to
excellence.

- Personal Life: In addition to his basketball career,
Kobe Bryant was a loving husband and father.
His tragic death in a helicopter crash in 2020 was
a profound loss for the sports world and beyond,
leaving a lasting legacy of determination and
passion.

MOTHER TERESA

- Date of Birth: August 26, 1910.
- Brief Biography: Mother Teresa, known as Saint
Teresa of Calcutta, was an Albanian-Indian
Roman Catholic nun and missionary. She devoted
her life to helping the poor, sick and needy in the
slums of India. She also founded the Missionaries
of Charity, a religious congregation.
- Virgo Traits: Compassionate and devoted to
serving others.
- Impact: Mother Teresa's selfless work and
dedication to the poor earned her worldwide
recognition. She was awarded the Nobel Peace
Prize in 1979 for her humanitarian efforts.

- Personal Life: Mother Teresa's life was dedicated to her religious calling and her mission to help those in need. Her work continues to inspire people around the world to selflessly serve others.

LYNDON B. JOHNSON

- Date of Birth: August 27, 1908.
- Brief Biography: Lyndon B. Johnson, often referred to as LBJ, was the 36th President of the United States, serving from 1963 to 1969. He played a pivotal role in advancing civil rights legislation and implementing his "Great Society" programs during his presidency.
- Virgo Traits: Strong work ethic and commitment to public service.
- Impact: Lyndon B. Johnson's presidency left a lasting impact on civil rights, education and healthcare.

- Personal Life: LBJ's personal life was marked by his dedication to public service. His presidency, while tumultuous, was defined by his commitment to social reform and the betterment of American society.

BEYONCE

- Date of Birth: September 4, 1981.
- Brief Biography: Beyoncé Knowles-Carter is an American singer, songwriter, actress and businesswoman. She rose to fame as a member of Destiny's Child and later pursued a highly successful solo career. Beyoncé is renowned for her powerful voice, dynamic performances and influence in the music industry.
- Virgo Traits: Strong work ethic, dedication to her craft and attention to detail.
- Impact: Beyoncé's impact on music and popular culture is immeasurable. She is celebrated for her vocal talent, stage presence and contributions to social justice through her art.
- Personal Life: Beyoncé is known for her privacy. She has been involved in various charitable endeavors and advocacy work. Her marriage to Jay-Z and their family life have garnered significant media attention.

CHARLIE SHEEN

- Date of Birth: September 3, 1965.
- Brief Biography: Charlie Sheen is an American actor known for his roles in films such as

"Platoon" and the television series "Two and a Half Men." He has been a prominent figure in both film and television throughout his career.

- Virgo Traits: Strong work ethic, particularly in his acting career.
- Impact: Charlie Sheen's career has had its share of highs and lows. His talent and charisma have made him a recognizable and influential figure in the entertainment industry.
- Personal Life: Sheen's personal life has been marked by controversies and public struggles, including issues with substance abuse. Despite these challenges, he remains a figure of interest in the world of entertainment.

COLONEL SANDERS

- Date of Birth: September 9, 1890.
- Brief Biography: Colonel Harland Sanders was an American businessman and the founder of Kentucky Fried Chicken (KFC). His famous recipe for fried chicken and his franchise system revolutionized the fast-food industry.
- Virgo Traits: Strong work ethic, particularly in building his business empire.
- Impact: Colonel Sanders' entrepreneurial spirit and dedication to his fried chicken recipe led to the worldwide success of KFC. His legacy endures through the global popularity of the brand.
- Personal Life: Sanders' life was centered around his business endeavors, and his dedication to

KFC made him an iconic figure in the fast-food industry.

AMY WINEHOUSE

- Date of Birth: September 14, 1983.
- Brief Biography: Amy Winehouse was an English singer and songwriter known for her distinctive voice. She achieved critical acclaim and commercial success during her brief career.
- Virgo Traits: Strong dedication to her music and songwriting. Attention to detail in her vocal delivery and compositions.
- Impact: Amy Winehouse's music left a lasting impact on the music industry. Her album "Back to Black" received widespread acclaim and recognition, earning her multiple Grammy Awards.
- Personal Life: Winehouse's personal life was marked by struggles with addiction and mental health issues. Her tragic death in 2011 at a young age was a profound loss to the music world.

AGATHA CHRISTIE

- Date of Birth: September 15, 1890.
- Brief Biography: Agatha Christie was an English writer known as the "Queen of Mystery." She authored numerous detective novels, short stories and plays. These include iconic works like "Murder on the Orient Express" and "Death on the Nile."

- Virgo Traits: Attention to detail in crafting intricate mysteries. Strong work ethic in producing a vast body of work.
- Impact: Agatha Christie's detective novels have captivated readers for generations. Her characters Hercule Poirot and Miss Marple have become iconic figures in the mystery genre.
- Personal Life: Christie's personal life was marked by her love of writing and her prolific output as an author. Her works continue to be celebrated in literature and adapted into various forms of media.

LARRY NELSON

- Date of Birth: August 10, 1947.
- Brief Biography: Larry Nelson is a retired American professional golfer known for his achievements in the sport. He won three major championships and had a successful career on the PGA Tour.
- Virgo Traits: Strong work ethic and dedication to golf.
- Impact: Larry Nelson's impact on professional golf is evident through his major championship victories and successful career. He is respected for his golfing abilities and contributions to the sport.
- Personal Life: Nelson's personal life revolves around his passion for golf. He continues to be involved in the sport as a course designer and commentator, sharing his expertise with the golfing community.

CAMERON DIAZ

- Date of Birth: August 30, 1972.
- Brief Biography: Cameron Diaz is an American actress, producer and author. She is well known for her roles in films such as "There's Something About Mary" and "Charlie's Angels."
- Virgo Traits: Strong work ethic and commitment to her acting career.
- Impact: Cameron Diaz's talent and charisma have made her a prominent figure in Hollywood. Her contributions to film and her versatile acting roles have garnered her wide spread recognition and acclaim.
- Personal Life: While Diaz has kept a relatively private personal life. She has been involved in various philanthropic endeavors and continues to be a beloved figure in the entertainment world.

These profiles offer a glimpse into the lives and traits of famous individuals born under the Virgo sign. They showcase their unique talents and contributions to various fields. While their journeys differ, they all exemplify the diligence, attention to detail and pursuit of excellence often associated with Virgo individuals.

From the glitz and glamor of Hollywood to the world's heights. From sports arenas, green fields to the enchanting melodies of music. Virgos have engraved their names in history. Their impact resonates not only in their fields but also in the hearts and minds of countless admirers worldwide.

As we celebrate the Virgo personalities showcased in this chapter we encourage you to draw inspiration from their journeys. Whether you share their birthdate or simply share a desire for excellence. Always remember that while stars may guide us it is your determination, work and attention to detail that will ultimately shape your path towards greatness.

Let the tales of these Virgo's serve as a reminder that striving for excellence and dedicating oneself to their chosen path with unwavering pursuit are qualities that lead to success. Embrace these attributes and may your own journey be just as extraordinary and motivating

CONCLUSION

As we draw the celestial curtain on this book dedicated to the Virgo star sign, we invite you to embark on one final exploration. One that summarizes the intricate tapestry that weaves through the lives of those born between August 23 and September 22. This concluding chapter serves as a celestial compass, guiding us through the key points and insights shared throughout the book.

In our journey through the world of Virgo, we've uncovered a rich tapestry of traits, influences and insights that define this zodiac sign. Let's now take a moment to revisit the key points and discoveries that have illuminated the Virgo personality.

- **The Pragmatic Perfectionist**: Virgos are known for their meticulous attention to detail and their relentless pursuit of perfection in all aspects of life, making them excellent problem-solvers and organizers.

- **The Earth Element:** As an Earth sign, Virgos are grounded, practical and deeply connected to the physical world. They find comfort in the tangible and often excel in hands-on tasks.

- **Mercury's Influence**: Mercury, the ruling planet of Virgo, bestows intellectual acumen, effective communication skills and a love for learning upon Virgo individuals.

- **Symbolism**: The symbol of the Virgin represents purity, virtue and a desire for order. Virgos seek to harmonize their inner and outer worlds.

- **Virgo in Love**: Virgo individuals approach love and relationships with thoughtfulness and care. They seek partners who appreciate their attention to detail and appreciate practical gestures of love.

- **Compatibility**: Virgos often find compatibility with Taurus, Capricorn and other Earth signs. Water signs like Cancer and Scorpio also connect well with them, balancing their practicality with emotional depth.

- **Challenges**: Virgos' pursuit of perfection can lead to self-criticism and anxiety. Learning to balance their high standards with self-compassion is essential for their well-being.

- **Friends and Family**: Virgos are loyal and dependable friends and family members. They value close relationships and often serve as anchors in their social circles.

- **Career and Money**: Virgos excel in careers that require attention to detail, problem-solving, and organization. Their strong work ethic often leads to financial stability and success.

- **Personal Growth**: Virgos can harness their analytical skills and practicality to achieve personal growth and self-improvement. Setting realistic goals and focusing on self-care are key to their development.

Throughout this book we've taken a journey to uncover what makes the Virgo zodiac sign unique. We've explored its history, delved into its personality traits and examined how Virgos handle various aspects of life. Including love and relationships, career choices, personal development and much more.

Our main goal has been to provide understanding and a roadmap for both Virgos themselves and those interested in this sign. We aim to highlight the nature of Virgo by emphasizing their strengths while addressing challenges they may face. Additionally we offer advice to help individuals close with the Virgo sign, thrive.

The core message of this book is crystal clear; Virgos stand out with their attention to detail, unwavering pursuit of excellence in all they do well. This in addition to their dedication, towards self improvement and caring for others. We encourage readers to embrace these qualities recognizing that they are not simply characteristics but powerful tools, for growth and fulfillment.

Ultimately this book showcases astrology as a perspective that helps us better understand ourselves and the world around us. It provides insights into the forces that shape our lives and promotes self awareness, self acceptance and personal development.

In conclusion we urge individuals born under the sign of Virgo to wholeheartedly embrace their qualities. Your dedication, practicality and attention to detail are attributes that can lead to great accomplishments and meaningful connections. By aligning your traits with your aspirations you can confidently navigate life's dance with purpose.

As we conclude this voyage remember that you are not confined by the stars; rather you are in control of your destiny. You are the captain steering your ship through the celestial seas. May the insights of Virgo and the influence of astrology inspire you to navigate a path of deep fulfillment and joy.

As we wrap up this exploration of the Virgo zodiac sign we find ourselves immersed in a realm of wisdom, groundedness and commitment. The sharp intellect and compassionate hearts of Virgos remind us that striving for perfection is not a fixed destination. Rathermore it is an ongoing journey towards self growth and self discovery.

In conclusion let us honor the presence of Virgo individuals in our lives and acknowledge the contributions they make to our world. Their unwavering dedication to excellence, meticulous attention to detail and boundless capacity for compassion are blessings that enrich our existence.

May this book serve as a guiding light, for both Virgos themselves and those seeking an understanding of them. As we bid farewell to this book may the wisdom associated with the Virgo sign continue to illuminate your path. May it lead you towards a life brimming with purpose, personal development and your own pursuit of excellence.

www.ingramcontent.com/pod-product-compliance
Lightning Source LLC
Chambersburg PA
CBHW072035150726

47999CB00002B/919